ABC ESSENTIALS

On a PATH of PRAYER

A navigation tool for an intimate prayer journey

LORI WAGNER

AFFIRMING FAITH
8900 Ortonville Road | Clarkston, MI 48348
www.affirmingfaith.org

© 2018 by Lori Wagner

ISBN: 978-0-9897373-8-8

All rights reserved. No portion of this publication may be reproduced, stored in an electronic system, or transmitted in any form or by any means, electronic, mechanical, photocopy, recording, or otherwise, without the prior permission of Affirming Faith. Requests for permission should be addressed in writing to Affirming Faith, 8900 Ortonville Road, Clarkston, MI 48348. Brief quotations may be used in literary reviews.

Scriptures, unless otherwise noted, are taken from the King James Bible, Public Domain.

Printed in the United States of America

DEDICATION

This book is dedicated to the incredible team of leaders and praying men and women who faithfully serve in the World Network of Prayer. Proceeds from this publication are designated for the support of this vital ministry.

ACKNOWLEDGEMENTS

Many thanks to Lisa Marshall and Colleen Clabaugh for their help with this project, and to Rev. Flo Shaw for her careful leadership of the World Network of Prayer.

Tremendous thanks, also, to those who faithfully uphold in prayer the ministry of Affirming Faith.

CONTENTS

PART I

Chapter 1:
In Prayer School with Jesus 9

Chapter 2
Prayer Principles & Applications 25

PART II

ABC Essentials on a Path of Prayer 33

Chapter 1

In Prayer School with Jesus

*Prayer is wonderful,
and prayer is work.*

No single book could provide a thorough teaching that explains every aspect and facet of prayer. After all, prayer is communing and communicating with a living God. Every encounter with the Lord brings with it the potential of an exciting new experience.

Prayer can also be a struggle. Many sincere, committed Christians find themselves desiring to develop their prayer lives but not quite knowing how. *ABC Essentials on a Path of Prayer* was created for this purpose—as a tool to help you bring depth and dimension to your personal devotions, and also as an aid in guiding group prayer.

PRAYER 101

When Jesus taught His disciples to pray, He began with the basics. His introductory lesson (commonly called "The Lord's Prayer") is found in his lengthier teaching, the "Sermon on the Mount."

Before Jesus began His instructions to the crowd in Matthew 6:9, He first made a significant point. Every believer should have a private prayer life.

Enter into thy closet and shut the door.
—Matt 6:6

Jesus certainly participated in and promoted group prayer, but with these words it's clear He wanted His followers to know the importance of having personal time with God.

The term "closet" has caused confusion to some. Jesus wasn't necessarily talking about a literal closet—a four-walled, windowless room. He meant that when people enter times of private prayer, they should shut themselves away from others. It's very helpful to have a designated place (and time) to pray. If you already do, you know the benefit. If this is a new concept to you, I'm confident you can find a "meeting place" that will become a peaceful refuge for you away from the distractions of family, ministry, work, or other obligations. When you step into that familiar place you will sense His presence waiting to meet you.

When you feel drawn to shut out the world but you aren't in your meeting place, simply close your eyes, and there you are—shut in with God. I've been known in worship services and times of public prayer to bury my face in a handkerchief. The simple act of closing myself off with a square of fabric gives me the feeling that I'm alone with Jesus in a sacred place. And it's a sweet place, indeed.

Let's look at the pattern of prayer Jesus presented His followers in Matt 6:9-13:

Our Father which art in heaven, Hallowed be thy name.
Thy kingdom come, Thy will be done in earth, as it is in heaven.
Give us this day our daily bread.
And forgive us our debts, as we forgive our debtors.
And lead us not into temptation, but deliver us from evil: For thine is the kingdom, and the power, and the glory, for ever. Amen.

The path of prayer Jesus outlined had two primary objectives:

1. Reveal the Father.
2. Teach the people to embrace God with a childlike faith.

Notice Jesus' approach:

- Start with relationship—*Our Father.*
- Profess God's holiness.
- Pray the kingdom of God would be established.
- Make requests for personal needs and relationships.
- Reaffirm His sovereign ability and glory.
- Agree with the promises of God.

We could spend many hours dissecting and learning from this pattern, and we will implement its principles as we move into the *ABC Essentials* later in this book, but the main point I want you to take from this familiar prayer is this: "The Lord's Prayer" is Jesus' *introductory* lesson. It was the prayer He taught the masses—even those who didn't fully realize who He was and those who didn't continue to develop deeper relationships with Him.

"The Lord's Prayer" was a great beginning, and this prayer remains the foundation on which to build an effective prayer life. Identifying it as Prayer 101 in no way minimizes its importance. Good teachers utilize a cycle of learning to effectively convey concepts. First they teach the basics, then loop back over them, review, circle higher, and build by adding more information on what was already taught. Consider, for example, how math tables are necessary to learn long division. Jesus wasn't finished teaching on prayer.

PRAYER 201

As the disciples walked with Jesus over the years that followed, they learned more about kingdom praying. Jesus took them from spiritual infancy to a more mature place of prayer.

We read about this in the gospel of Mark. Jesus had commissioned his disciples to go out and minister among the people in His name. They did as He said, and they saw results, but there came a time their effectiveness reached an impasse. A spirit would not yield to their words alone. Jesus told them why. He said,

This kind can come forth by nothing, but by prayer and fasting.
—Mark 9:29

Prayer 201 introduces the discipline of fasting as an empowerment to prayer. Refraining from eating and/or drinking, whether done corporately or not, is always a private matter. The disciples had ministered two-by-two, but fasting will always be between you and your flesh.

Although scripturally fasting clearly refers to food and beverages, a broader concept applies that could include other areas of our lives:

> IF WE WANT TO SEE GREATER RESULTS, WE MUST OFFER GREATER CONSECRATIONS.

Denying the body food or water in and of itself doesn't force God's hand to move on a person's behalf—that would be manipulation, and God will not be manipulated. Fasting does, however, humble the soul; and true humility gets God's attention.

If my people, which are called by my name, shall humble themselves, and pray, and seek my face, and turn from their wicked ways; then will I

hear from heaven, and will forgive their sin, and will heal their land.
—2 Chr 7:14

The primary purpose of fasting is to shut down human appetites for the things of the flesh and make believers more sensitive to the things of the Spirit. Fasting fine-tunes human spirits to hear the voice of God.

The greatest benefit of fasting is the relationship it develops between a believer and God. The relationship that cultivates as a result of fasting is the key to powerful, answered prayers.

Scripture reveals a hierarchy of evil powers, and to see the many levels of the kingdom of the enemy fall requires empowerment from the kingdom of heaven that comes through consecrated living and communion with God. On the basis of a believer's relationship with the Lord, he or she is authorized to cast out spiritual darkness and move mountains in Jesus' name.

ADVANCED TRAINING

Beyond childhood and adolescence (the transitional and training years), Jesus eventually challenged His disciples to "grow up." It began with one incredible word: *hitherto*.

Before His crucifixion and death, Jesus gave His disciples their last instructions.

And in that day ye shall ask me nothing. Verily, verily, I say unto you, Whatsoever ye shall ask the Father in my name, he will give it you.

Hitherto have ye asked nothing in my name: ask, and ye shall receive, that your joy may be full.
—John 16:23–24

As we noted previously, in the early days of the disciples' ministry His followers used the authority of Jesus' name to cast out devils and heal the sick. They understood this authority to be from the Messiah—the man, Christ Jesus. No doubt they recognized it as power from heaven, but what we do not see before this time is the disciples making kingdom requests of God in Jesus' name. They operated in the authority of the Messiah—the Son of Man who walked among them.

Up to this point, we see a picture of the disciples moving out, testing the authority Jesus imparted to them. They operated on the Lord's behalf, yet Jesus knew they lacked what they would need when He was no longer walking beside them in bodily form. With the future of the church in mind, Jesus gave His disciples a two-levered key that would open the door on a new way to live and minister.

The two levers (or lifters) of that key were these—a principle and a promise.

THE PRINCIPLE

Believers will be permitted and even invited to speak directly to the God of heaven and earth when they pray in Jesus' name.

THE POWER

God will individually fill those who trust in Him according to His Word with the same dynamic Spirit that spoke the world into existence and raised Jesus from the dead.

Before His arrest and crucifixion, Jesus spoke His last words to His disciples. In them, He gave them these "prayer promises" we just discussed, and He began by saying, "In that day" (see John 16:23).

He assured His disciples that from "that day"—a specific, designated point in time—they would no longer need to ask Him, the man Christ Jesus, anything. They may not have fully understood the depths of what He spoke to them then, but looking back, it's clear Jesus was speaking of personal access to the presence of God. The sacrifice He would make as a substitution for the offence of mankind would remove the divide between deity and humanity. Whosoever would believe and turn to Him could receive spiritual rebirth (see Acts 2:38). The door to the presence of God would be opened by the blood and in the name of Jesus. What was this very important day?

Jesus was referring to the day of Pentecost. He was speaking about what would happen after His Spirit came and filled the believers (see Acts 1:8). Jesus commanded His disciples to wait for the power that would come from heaven—and come it did (see Acts

2:4). That same power and authority in prayer is available to every believer filled with the Spirit of God, and every believer must experience Pentecost to access the fullness of what Christ suffered on Calvary to give them.

After the work of the cross, and because of their faith and obedience, Jesus' followers received power from on high. With the indwelling Spirit and the fullness of the stature of mature believers, the disciples were empowered to pray in a new way. They could now ask, seek, knock, and receive from the Father when they prayed in Jesus' name. This is a heritage for every Spirit-filled believer who prays in the will of God.

MORE "HITHERTOS"

In addition to Jesus' "hitherto," the apostle Paul also used the word when speaking to believers in the church. He was not pleased the Christians in Corinth had failed to progress in the development of their faith. He said,

I have fed you with milk, and not with meat: for hitherto ye were not able to bear it, neither yet now are ye able.
—1 Cor 3:2

Paul corrected the church for their willingness to remain spiritually immature—fed with milk and not meat. It's God's expressed desire that His people grow from precept to precept and from glory to glory.

> IT'S NOT GOD'S WILL THAT
> HIS PEOPLE CHOOSE TO
> REMAIN ON THE IMMATURE
> SIDE OF "HITHERTO."

"Hitherto" is a "hinge" of sorts. It marks the place where things changed, will change, or should change. A "hitherto" has a "before," a "not as yet," or a "not until now." But the very presence of the word indicates a hoped-for transition.

In these last days God is calling men, women, and churches to a "hitherto." He has in mind a "hitherto" for you—and something wonderful hangs on the other side of the "hinge of hitherto." Pentecost opened a door, and believers everywhere are invited to its threshold to ask, seek, knock, and see God answer as they pray in agreement with His will, His Word, and His Spirit.

You may have walked "this way" for years, but after a "hitherto" encounter with the Spirit, you can move into a new dimension. You can live in an "after today" moment and find yourself on the other side of the "hinge of hitherto" in your prayer life and walk with God.

It's time to grow up, saint of God. Eat the meat. Pray the prayer. And it's my sincere desire the tools in this book will benefit you in the same way they have encouraged and equipped me since I began this study ten months ago.

Chapter 2

Prayer Principles & Applications

*All prayer is valuable,
and every Christian should pray.*

Is prayer tedious for you? Challenging? Do you feel inadequate or lose your focus? There's good news! You don't have to pray like someone else for God to hear your prayers. In fact, from one day to the next, your prayers may not sound like they were coming from the same person. Some days you may pray with eloquence and other days you may falter. One moment you might whisper a heart-felt petition, and only a few minutes find yourself making bold declarations.

Prayer looks different and sounds different at any given time. There's not a "wrong" prayer or a "right" prayer. But know this: God wants to hear from you right where you are.

- One day your prayer may look like the Publican who struck his chest and cried out, "God be merciful to me a sinner" (see Luke 18:13).

- Another time your prayers may resemble those made by Hannah. She prayed with no audible words, but her emotion and body language caused the priest who observed her to believe she was drunk (see 1 Sam 1:12–13).

- It's possible you will pray at times with no discernible words, just sounds—even groanings (see Rom 8:26).

- In everyday life, you will experience moments when the only prayer you have time to pray is the name of Jesus (see Ps 50:15).
- In prayer you may use tools such as lists, cards, and visuals; and other times "free-style" in the Spirit (see 1 Cor 14:15).

There are varying types of prayer—different paths, courses, and depths of prayer. As you pray, and as you are led by the Spirit, the Lord will direct you through unseen gates. You will learn to approach Him in different ways on unique paths of prayer, supplication, intercession, and praises.

A HOUSE OF PRAYER

"Mine house shall be called a house of prayer for all people." This familiar saying was first recorded in the Old Testament and echoed in the New. Jesus quoted this prophecy from the writings of Isaiah. What is commonly missed, however, is that the phrase is not a "stand-alone" statement. It is the last part of a verse that speaks of God bringing into His kingdom people from every nation.

Even them will I bring to my holy mountain, and make them joyful in my house of prayer: their burnt offerings and their sacrifices shall be accepted upon mine altar; for mine house shall be called an house of prayer for all people.
—Isa 56:7

What did God say He would do for all His people from every tribe, kindred, and tongue? The Lord said He would "make them joyful" in His "house of prayer."

Isn't that beautiful? Yes, there are times we cry and pray and make our petitions. We worship—and worship is warfare. But what I want to bring to your attention as you read these words is the result of being in His house of prayer. God's great desire and intention in all your communion with Him is that He would make you joyful—joyful in His house of prayer. You don't even have to try. He said He would do it. That's just the way He runs His household.

YES, BUT HOW?

It sounds great, doesn't it? But perhaps you still have questions:

- How do I "enter in?"
- How do I journey into deeper prayer?
- Can I learn to access open gates and everlasting doors and pray in God's will?
- Can I truly move into a deeper dimension of prayer?
- What hinders me from going boldly to the throne of grace?
- How can I overcome hindrances and pray with confidence that He hears and will answer?

Some people come to prayer with guilt because they don't see themselves as forgiven and restored. Others leave prayer with guilt because they believe they haven't prayed long enough, hard enough, eloquent enough, or anointed enough.

It's time to lay aside any guilt or condemnation and realize God *wants* you to pray. If it's a quick prayer, a short prayer, a desperate prayer, a fellowship prayer, a blessing prayer, an intercessory prayer—whatever prayer you pray, God wants to hear.

The enemy wants you to feel guilty and condemned so you won't pray. Or he wants you to consider yourself so unworthy you enter prayer with your tail tucked in. That is *not* walking in the authority God gave you to move mountains and shake the heavens.

HELP IS HERE!

In January of 2018, with my pastor's approval, I called an all-night-prayer meeting for our local church. My initial idea was to simply open the church, put on some background worship music, and let people pray. But in my prayer room at home, I felt very impressed that many of the people (including me) would need help.

For those who weren't accustomed to praying for long periods of time, how could I help them? Of course, if you want to learn to pray, go sit, kneel, or stand by someone who knows how to pray and learn to pray by following that person's lead. We learn to pray by praying, after all. But in preparation for that all-night prayer, I developed a pamphlet I called *ABC Essentials on a Path of Prayer.*

The book you are reading is a modification of that resource. Before you enter on your prayer journey, I want you to know you don't have to include every "step" to have an incredible time of prayer. This is a navigational tool that is meant to provide you with assistance—some pavers on a walkway, if you will.

It's a progressive journey, and as you engage in your individual prayer time, the Lord may veer you "off course" in a direction you aren't expecting. You may take "two steps" one direction, and the Lord might say, "Whoa. Stop there. We're just worshipping today." Or there may be some incredible need and the Holy Ghost calls you quickly to intercession.

There's no wrong way to pray if you have a right approach, and that is entering His presence through the first and only gate—the door—the shed blood of Jesus. Through repentance and acceptance of His sacrifice, and with thanksgiving, you can boldly enter His presence.

As you move into prayer, don't feel you need to stay in one position. Feel free to move. Allow the Lord to lead you as you take a prayer journey with Him from the gate of praise into the secret place of His presence.

PART II

ABC Essentials on a Path of Prayer

ACKNOWLEDGE God. Acknowledge His sovereignty, His majesty, His fatherhood of every nation, tribe, and tongue. **ACCESS** His presence with thanksgiving and praise. **ASK** Him to lead you in prayer.

Enter into his gates with thanksgiving, and into his courts with praise: be thankful unto him, and bless his name. —Ps 100:4

Lord, teach us to pray. —Luke 11:1

In all thy ways acknowledge him, and he shall direct thy paths. —Prov 3:6

 **BLESS** the Lord! Bless His holy Name! Bless His people. Bless your family. Bless your community. Bless yourself.

Bless the LORD, O my soul: and all that is within me, bless his holy name. —Ps 103:1

Not rendering evil for evil, or railing for railing: but contrariwise blessing; knowing that ye are thereunto called, that ye should inherit a blessing. —1 Pet 3:9

The LORD bless thee, and keep thee: The LORD make his face shine upon thee, and be gracious unto thee: The LORD lift up his countenance upon thee, and give thee peace. —Num 6:24–26

CONFESS your failures, frailty, and sins. Confess your dependence on God and humble yourself before the Lord. **COME** boldly to prayer, free from sin, guilt, and shame knowing Jesus enjoys your boldness.

Let us therefore come boldly unto the throne of grace, that we may obtain mercy, and find grace to help in time of need. —Heb 4:16

O Lord, hear; O Lord, forgive; O Lord, hearken and do; defer not, for thine own sake, O my God: for thy city and thy people are called by thy name. —Dan 9:19

The sacrifice of the wicked is an abomination to the LORD: but the prayer of the upright is his delight. —Prov 15:8

DESIRE Him, His will, His presence. Desire to understand His Word, His mission, plans, and strategies. **DELIGHT in Him**. Give Him your full attention.

Whom have I in heaven but thee? and there is none upon earth that I desire beside thee. —Ps 73:25

Delight thyself also in the LORD: and he shall give thee the desires of thine heart. —Ps 37:4

Surely the Lord GOD will do nothing, but he revealeth his secret unto his servants the prophets. —Amos 3:7

EXPRESS your prayers in English. Pray with understanding for known needs such as illness, relationships, financial needs, and emotional healing. Be **EXPLICIT** with your requests. Remember to pray for church and secular leadership.

I will pray with the spirit, and I will pray with the understanding also. —1 Cor 14:15

Give us this day our daily bread. —Matt 6:11

I exhort therefore, that, first of all, supplications, prayers, intercessions, and giving of thanks, be made for all men; For kings, and for all that are in authority; that we may lead a quiet and peaceable life in all godliness and honesty. —1 Tim 2:1–2

FUEL your prayers with FAITH knowing God wants you to pray. He's expecting you to pray. Pray believing in the object of your faith—the Lord Jesus. He is able and will answer prayer consistent with His Word and will. He is faithful and not limited by any circumstance.

And all things, whatsoever ye shall ask in prayer, believing, ye shall receive. —Matt 21:22

But without faith it is impossible to please him: for he that cometh to God must believe that he is, and that he is a rewarder of them that diligently seek him. —Heb 11:6

Beloved, if our heart condemn us not, then have we confidence toward God. And whatsoever we ask, we receive of him, because we keep his commandments, and do those things that are pleasing in his sight. —1 John 3:21–22

GIVE God the glory for who He is and all He's done. Praise Him for every promise He's made and kept. Take a praise break and give thanks to the Lord, for He is good.

Not unto us, O LORD, not unto us, but unto thy name give glory, for thy mercy, and for thy truth's sake. —Ps 115:1

O give thanks unto the LORD; for he is good; for his mercy endureth for ever. —1 Chr 16:34

In every thing give thanks: for this is the will of God in Christ Jesus concerning you. —1 Thess 5:18

HEAR His voice. Stop and listen to His personal words to you, the impressions in your spirit.

Shew me thy ways, O LORD; teach me thy paths. Lead me in thy truth, and teach me: for thou art the God of my salvation; on thee do I wait all the day. —Ps 25:4–5

LORD, thou hast heard the desire of the humble: thou wilt prepare their heart, thou wilt cause thine ear to hear. —Ps 10:17

Call unto me, and I will answer thee, and show thee great and mighty things, which thou knowest not. —Jer 33:3

INVOKE the name of Jesus! His power and authority! Proclaim what the name of Jesus means to you personally. Speak it out. Fortify your mind in the strong tower of His name.

And whatsoever ye shall ask in my name, that will I do, that the Father may be glorified in the Son. If ye shall ask any thing in my name, I will do it. —John 14:13-14

Wherefore God also hath highly exalted him, and given him a name which is above every name: That at the name of Jesus every knee should bow, of things in heaven, and things in earth, and things under the earth. —Phil 2:9-10

The name of the LORD is a strong tower: the righteous runneth into it, and is safe. —Prov 18:10

JUDGE your motives and actions.

Make a self-examination and ask God to help you discern where you are in your Christian walk. You are in training. Allow God to judge your heart and point out anything that needs correction and development.

For if we would judge ourselves, we should not be judged. —1 Cor 11:31

Thus saith the LORD of hosts; Consider your ways. —Hag 1:7

Thou hypocrite, first cast out the beam out of thine own eye; and then shalt thou see clearly to cast out the mote out of thy brother's eye. —Matt 7:5

KNOCK. God is your friend, and He is a God of abundant resources. He invited you to ask, seek and knock. **KNOCK** until you touch God—until you feel the door open and the need being met.

And I say unto you, Ask, and it shall be given you; seek, and ye shall find; knock, and it shall be opened unto you. —Luke 11:8

Continue in prayer, and watch in the same with thanksgiving; Withal praying also for us, that God would open unto us a door of utterance, to speak the mystery of Christ, for which I am also in bonds. —Col 4:2-3

Hear, O LORD, when I cry with my voice: have mercy also upon me, and answer me.
—Ps 27:7

LIFT praise to the Lord. Be demonstrative and praise Him with all your heart, soul, mind, and strength. **LEAP for joy** if you are able—for your great reward (the presence of God) is with you when you praise Him.

Rejoice, and be exceeding glad: for great is your reward in heaven. —Matt 5:12

And as the ark of the LORD came into the city of David, Michal Saul's daughter looked through a window, and saw king David leaping and dancing before the LORD; and she despised him in her heart. —2 Sam 6:16

And there came a fire out from before the LORD, and consumed upon the altar the burnt offering and the fat: which when all the people saw, they shouted, and fell on their faces.
—Lev 9:24

MEDITATE on God's word, ways, gifts, and callings in your life. Ask the Lord to lead your thoughts and give you the mind of Christ —to instill His words in your spirit. Harmonize your thoughts with His by bringing them into agreement with His written Word. Also agree in prayer with words you have received directly from Him and through trusted leaders.

Gird up the loins of your mind, be sober, and hope to the end for the grace that is to be brought unto you at the revelation of Jesus Christ.
—1 Pet 1:13

Till I come, give attendance to reading, to exhortation, to doctrine. Meditate upon these things; give thyself wholly to them; that thy profiting may appear to all. —1 Tim 4:13, 15

Let this mind be in you, which was also in Christ Jesus. —Phil 2:5

 **NOTE** the people and situations God brought to your attention in prayer. Refer to any notes you have made of previous prayer requests. Make note of anything pertinent that came to you in your time of meditation.

Thus speaketh the LORD God of Israel, saying, Write thee all the words that I have spoken unto thee. —Jer 30:2

And the LORD answered me, and said, Write the vision, and make it plain upon tables, that he may run that readeth it. —Hab 2:2

Brethren, pray for us. —1 Thess 5:25

OFFER prayers of intercession for those who don't know the Lord—at home and abroad. Intercede for those who have walked away from Him and those who are struggling. See yourself at the altar of incense and lift your prayers and supplications as a fragrant offering before the throne of God.

To open their eyes, and to turn them from darkness to light, and from the power of Satan unto God, that they may receive forgiveness of sins, and inheritance among them which are sanctified by faith that is in me. —Acts 26:18

Mine eye runneth down with rivers of water for the destruction of the daughter of my people. Mine eye trickleth down, and ceaseth not, without any intermission. Till the Lord look down, and behold from heaven. —Lam 3:48–50

My heart's desire and prayer to God for Israel is, that they might be saved. —Rom 10:1

PRAY in the Spirit. God's Spirit will help you pray specific needs for revival, conviction, and divine intervention. Step in the gap for others. Pull down strongholds of spiritual wickedness.

But ye, beloved, building up yourselves on your most holy faith, praying in the Holy Ghost.
—Jude 20

And the Lord said, If ye had faith as a grain of mustard seed, ye might say unto this sycamine tree, Be thou plucked up by the root, and be thou planted in the sea; and it should obey you.
— Luke 17:6

Likewise the Spirit also helpeth our infirmities: for we know not what we should pray for as we ought: but the Spirit itself maketh intercession for us with groanings which cannot be uttered. —Rom 8:26

QUERY God. Ask the Lord for His instructions on how to pray further. Ask for His strategies as you seek to participate in His plans and His will. **QUOTE Scripture.**

For this cause we also, since the day we heard it, do not cease to pray for you, and to desire that ye might be filled with the knowledge of his will in all wisdom and spiritual understanding. —Col 1:9

Now when ... they were forbidden of the Holy Ghost to preach the word in Asia ... a vision appeared to Paul in the night; There stood a man of Macedonia, and prayed him, saying, Come over into Macedonia, and help us. —Acts 16:6–10

For the word of God is quick, and powerful, and sharper than any twoedged sword, piercing even to the dividing asunder of soul and spirit, and of the joints and marrow, and is a discerner of the thoughts and intents of the heart. —Heb 4:12

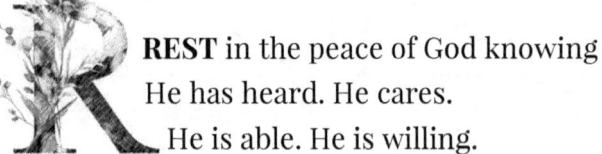

REST in the peace of God knowing He has heard. He cares. He is able. He is willing.

And he said, My presence shall go with thee, and I will give thee rest. —Exod 33:14

Thou wilt keep him in perfect peace, whose mind is stayed on thee: because he trusteth in thee. —Isa 26:3

He maketh me to lie down in green pastures: he leadeth me beside the still waters. He restoreth my soul: he leadeth me in the paths of righteousness for his name's sake. —Ps 23:2-3

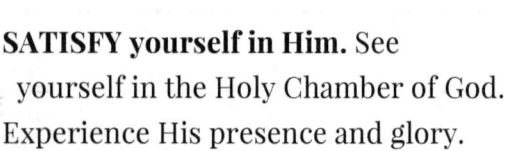

SATISFY yourself in Him. See yourself in the Holy Chamber of God. Experience His presence and glory. **SING** to Him and hear Him sing over you.

Blessed is the man whom thou choosest, and causest to approach unto thee, that he may dwell in thy courts: we shall be satisfied with the goodness of thy house, even of thy holy temple.
—Ps 65:4

For he satisfieth the longing soul, and filleth the hungry soul with goodness. —Ps 107:9

Thou wilt shew me the path of life: in thy presence is fulness of joy; at thy right hand there are pleasures for evermore. —Ps 16:11

The LORD thy God in the midst of thee is mighty; he will save, he will rejoice over thee with joy; he will rest in his love, he will joy over thee with singing. —Zeph 3:17

TURN your eyes upon Jesus. It's all about Him—the lover of your soul. He is your Bridegroom full of love and passion for you. Linger in the pavilion of His presence.

But he, being full of the Holy Ghost, looked up stedfastly into heaven, and saw the glory of God, and Jesus standing on the right hand of God. —Acts 7:55

How amiable are thy tabernacles, O LORD of hosts. My soul longeth, yea, even fainteth for the courts of the LORD: my heart and my flesh crieth out for the living God. —Ps 84:1-2

His mouth is most sweet: yea, he is altogether lovely. This is my beloved, and this is my friend, O daughters of Jerusalem. —Song 5:16

UNCOVER yourself before the Lord. Grant Him all access to every part of you. He knows everything about you and loves you beyond measure. Give yourself to Him and receive the weight of His glory upon you.

Neither is there any creature that is not manifest in his sight: but all things are naked and opened unto the eyes of him with whom we have to do. —Heb 4:13

And thou shalt love the LORD thy God with all thine heart, and with all thy soul, and with all thy might. —Deut 6:5

Whom having not seen, ye love; in whom, though now ye see him not, yet believing, ye rejoice with joy unspeakable and full of glory. — 1 Pet 5:8

VENTURE where you've not gone before. Ask God to lead you into a deeper prayer experience with Him—richer, broader, more mature and kingdom focused. Trust Him to lead you.

And to know the love of Christ, which passeth knowledge, that ye might be filled with all the fulness of God. —Eph 3:19

I have shewed thee new things from this time, even hidden things, and thou didst not know them. —Isa 48:6

Oh how great is thy goodness, which thou hast laid up for them that fear thee; which thou hast wrought for them that trust in thee before the sons of men! —Ps 31:19

WORSHIP the Lord in the beauty of holiness. Go beyond praise that takes you to God and give Him an absolute devotion that draws Him to you. Focus everything on Him.

My soul doth magnify the Lord, And my spirit hath rejoiced in God my Saviour.
—Luke 1:46–47

In the year that king Uzziah died I saw also the Lord sitting upon a throne, high and lifted up, and his train filled the temple. Above it stood the seraphims.... And one cried unto another, and said, Holy, holy, holy, is the Lord of hosts: the whole earth is full of his glory. —Isa 6:1-3

Give unto the Lord the glory due unto his name: bring an offering, and come before him: worship the Lord in the beauty of holiness.
—1 Chr 16:29

EXTOL the one who lifted you out of sin and into abundant life. **EXALT** the Lord your God.

I will extol thee, O LORD; for thou hast lifted me up, and hast not made my foes to rejoice over me. —Ps 30:1

Sing unto God, sing praises to his name: extol him that rideth upon the heavens by his name JAH, and rejoice before him. —Ps 68:4

The LORD liveth; and blessed be my rock; and let the God of my salvation be exalted.
—Ps 18:46

YIELD yourself. Surrender all of yourself to God—your will, your future, your desires, thoughts, relationships, career, ministry, and opinions. Consecrate yourself to Him as a servant of righteousness. Say **YES**!

Neither yield ye your members as instruments of unrighteousness unto sin: but yield yourselves unto God...and your members as instruments of righteousness unto God. —Rom 6:13

For Moses had said, Consecrate yourselves today to the LORD, even every man upon his son, and upon his brother; that he may bestow upon you a blessing this day. —Exod 32:29

For as ye have yielded your members servants to uncleanness and to iniquity unto iniquity; even so now yield your members servants to righteousness unto holiness. —Rom 6:19

ZEALOUSLY apply and pursue all God has shown you. Obey quickly. Be a channel of His love, grace, and influence in your world.

He shall have it, and his seed after him, even the covenant of an everlasting priesthood; because he was zealous for his God. —Num 25:13

Who gave himself for us, that he might redeem us from all iniquity, and purify unto himself a peculiar people, zealous of good works. —Titus 2:14

I delight to do thy will, O my God: yea, thy law is within my heart. —Ps 40:8

And they went forth, and preached every where, the Lord working with them, and confirming the word with them, and confirming the word with signs following. Amen. —Mark 16:20

Notes, Prayer Requests & Answered Prayers

Notes, Prayer Requests & Answered Prayers

_____
_____
_____
_____
_____
_____
_____
_____
_____
_____
_____
_____
_____

Notes, Prayer Requests & Answered Prayers

Notes, Prayer Requests & Answered Prayers

_____

_____

_____

_____

_____

_____

_____

_____

_____

_____

_____

_____

Notes, Prayer Requests & Answered Prayers

Notes, Prayer Requests & Answered Prayers

Notes, Prayer Requests & Answered Prayers

For additional resources by Lori Wagner visit
www.affirmingfaith.org

Through the Waters: The Life & Ministry of Evangelist Willie Johnson

Holy Intimacy

Preach Like a Lady

Gender & Ministry

Wisdom is a Lady

Arise! Walk in the Sunrise!

The Scent of Hope

Quilting Patches of Life

A Patchwork of Freedom

Gates & Fences: Straight Talk in a Crooked World

Christian 101

The 8 Days of Christmas

Gateway to the Sun

Bachik the Birthday Kiss

The Pure Path Series:
The Girl in the Dress, Covered by Love, Unmasked, The Pure Life

Historical Fiction Trilogy:
The Rose of Sharon, Buttercup & Marigold

Orbis, The Fun Family Game You Win by Blessing Your World

www.ingramcontent.com/pod-product-compliance
Lightning Source LLC
Chambersburg PA
CBHW070437010526
44118CB00014B/2078